The Gruesome Truth About

The Middle Ages

Written by

Jillian Powell

Illustrated by

Matt Buckingham

D0320640

34 4124 0004 1349

Published by Wayland in 2012

Wayland
338 Euston Road
London NW1 3BH

Wayland Australia
Level 17/207 Kent Street
Sydney NSW 2000

All rights reserved.

Editor: Victoria Brooker
Design: billybooks.co.uk
Consultant: Martyn Whittock, Head of History and
Director of Humanities Faculty, Kingdown School,
Warminster, Wiltshire.
British Library Cataloguing in Publication Data
Powell, Jillian
The gruesome truth about the Middle Ages.
1. Middle Ages--Juvenile literature.
I. Title II. Middle Ages
909'.07-dc22

ISBN 978 0 7502 6796 0

This paperback edition published in 2012 by Wayland
Reprinted by Wayland in 2012
Text copyright © Wayland 2010
Illustration copyright © Matt Buckingham 2010

Printed in China

Wayland is a division of Hachette Children's Books,
an Hachette UK company.
www.hachette.co.uk

Contents

The Marvellous Middle Ages

▲ Warwick Castle dates from the 13th and 14th centuries and was home to the Earls of Warwick.

The years from around 1000 to 1500 CE in Europe are known as the Middle Ages, or the Medieval period. It was a time when cities and towns were growing fast and farming was improving with the invention of new methods and tools. The first hospitals and universities were built and the first printed books appeared with the invention of the printing press in Germany in the mid 1400s.

The Middle Ages produced great poetry, such as the works of Chaucer and Malory, as well as beautiful architecture, including grand stone castles, abbeys and cathedrals. Skilled craftsmen made sculptures, wall paintings, **illuminated manuscripts** and stained glass windows to decorate them.

▲ William Caxton founded the first printing press in England in 1476.

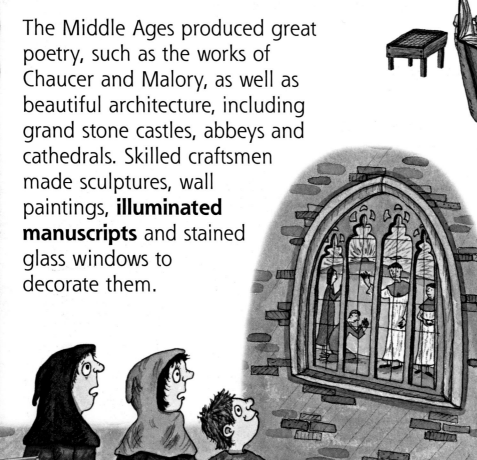

◀ Stained glass windows told stories from the Bible when many people could not read.

Gruesome truth

Those are some of the things that you probably already know about the Middle Ages, but in this book you'll find out the gory and grisly bits that no one ever tells you! Each double page will begin with a well-known FACT, before going on to tell you the gruesome truth. Look out for these features throughout the book – the answers are on page 32.

WHAT IS IT? Guess the mystery object.

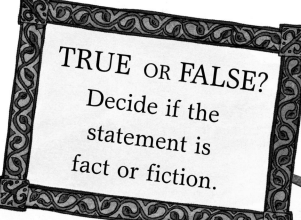

TRUE OR FALSE? Decide if the statement is fact or fiction.

Maps and monsters

Medieval treasures include the Hereford Mappa Mundi, which shows us how people saw the world in the 13th century. Mapmakers drew these early maps by hand and often included places named in the Bible like the Garden of Eden, as well as fantastical creatures and monsters in faraway lands.

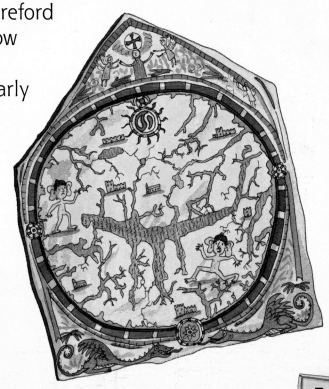

▶ The Mappa Mundi includes an imaginary people who wrapped themselves in their huge ears to keep warm, and a creature called a Sciapod that sheltered from the sun under its single enormous foot.

Dingy Dwellings

FACT Medieval homes ranged from grand castles built from stone to manor houses and cottages built on frames of oak.

▼ Stone or earth floors were covered with loose straw. The straw often needed to be swept out and replaced or it became dirty and smelly with spills, crumbs and bugs.

Gruesome truth

Many people lived in cramped, dark cottages, which had walls made from straw, mud and cow dung. Peasants' cottages had only one or two rooms, with a space at one end for the farm animals that were brought inside at night.

Smoke and shutters

Few people could afford window glass and most homes just had small holes in the walls with wooden shutters that made it dark inside when they were closed. The only light came from smoky fires and candles made from animal fat.

Only the palaces of the royals and nobles had bathrooms. Most people managed with wooden buckets and barrels of water and slept on straw mattresses that were full of lice and bed bugs.

▼ Poor families often had to share a bed.

Public privies

Toilets – called privies – were just a stone or wooden seat over a hole or pit. Some castles had privies in small towers or outhouses set outside the walls that emptied through a hole or shaft into a **cesspit** or **moat**. Others emptied into a river, or just into the street. The rich used cloth rags instead of toilet paper. Poorer people made do with hay or leaves.

WHAT IS IT?

▶ Toilets in turrets emptied through shafts or just holes in the floor. Some medieval pictures show this happening!

Herbs and Hygiene

FACT Medieval people believed washing would keep the **soul** as well as the body clean. They often took baths and made their own soap, shampoo and toothpaste.

▼ In winter, people placed bath barrels by an open fire for warmth.

Gruesome truth

Most people had to bath in an old barrel with the top cut off. They had to fetch water from wells and heat it with firewood before filling the barrel. Sometimes, the whole family had to use the same bathwater.

Soap and stews

London had its own public baths called stews, which were bathing pools near the River Thames. People washed with soap made from wood ash mixed with animal fat. For their hair, they mixed up wood or fern ash with egg white or made a conditioner from boiled lizards. Hair removers for unwanted body hair were made with **quick lime** and poisonous arsenic.

▲ Sometimes thieves made off with people's clothes while they were bathing in the stews.

Cloth and bones

People cleaned their teeth with twigs and bits of woollen cloth, and sometimes a paste made from herbs, or ground up coral or **cuttlefish** bones. They chewed mint and birch leaves to sweeten their breath. Barber surgeons pulled out teeth when they went bad. Rich people could have false teeth, either human teeth or teeth made from cow bones.

WHAT IS IT?

▲ To get the high forehead popular in the 1400s, women plucked their hair, wore bandages soaked in vinegar and cat's dung, or rubbed walnut oil into the skin.

▶ Families stored their wee and women used it for soaking and cleaning clothes. The **ammonia** in the wee helped to loosen dirt and grime.

9

Weary Workers

FACT In the Middle Ages, everyone had their place in a **feudal** society, from the king at the top to the peasants at the bottom.

Gruesome truth

Feudal rules dictated what everyone from a lord to a peasant could or could not do. Peasants were the property of their Lord of the Manor. They lived short, hard lives with little freedom. They had to work on the land every day except for holy days and Sundays, and from the little they earned they had to pay taxes to the lord and to the church.

▲ Peasants had to swear to obey the Lord of the Manor on the Bible. They could not marry or leave the manor without his permission.

▲ The ranks of feudal society: king, knight, freeman and peasant. The king, his nobles and knights protected the people in return for their work on the land and the payment of taxes.

▼ Harrows broke up the earth after ploughing.

Horses and harrows

Peasants rented a small piece of land from the Lord of the Manor but they also had to farm his land and land owned by the church. Most people worked from morning to night, hoeing, muck-spreading, ploughing and harvesting using only simple hand tools like **scythes** and **harrows** and oxen and horses to help them. They had to pay the Lord of the Manor every time they needed to use his mill to grind their flour or his oven to bake their bread. They even had to pay him when their son was born or their daughter was married!

WHAT IS IT?

▶ Peasants had to give the church a tenth of what they produced each year, such as wool, honey, chickens or firewood.

Working Children

FACT Few children went to school in the Middle Ages. Boys from rich families went to private schools or were taught at home by a tutor. There were also some parish schools run by parish priests that taught children to read and write.

Gruesome truth

Most children had to work from the age of five years old. They helped at home and out in the fields, doing jobs like fetching water from wells, herding geese or sheep and gathering firewood.

▼ Children were sent out to gather firewood needed for cooking, heating and washing.

Scarecrows and servants

Even small children worked on the land, clearing stones or acting as scarecrows, to chase birds away from seeds and crops. Some worked as ploughboys. They had to walk alongside the oxen pulling a plough from daybreak until evening, using a long pole to keep them in line. Others were sent away to work as servants for rich families.

◄ Plough boys worked with a long pole called a perch.

Monks and masters

At the age of about 12 or 13, many boys were **apprenticed** to a trade for ten years. They became the property of their master who could sell them on. Children could also be sent away from home to become a monk or a nun.

▲ Boys apprenticed to a barrel maker were sometimes welcomed to the trade by being covered in treacle and rolled around in a barrel!

TRUE OR FALSE?
Babies were given dirty dishwater to drink.

▶ Kennel boys looked after a family's hunting dogs. They often had to sleep in a hayloft above the kennels.

13

Boars and Bustards

FACT In the Middle Ages, fresh foods were sold on markets and street stalls, and alehouses and cook shops provided hot meals and takeaways.

Gruesome truth

Favourite take-away foods included roasted song thrushes (two for a penny) and sheep's feet.

▲ Sheep's feet and pigs' trotters were popular dishes.

Bad bakers

In Medieval towns and cities, some bakers cheated their customers, either by adding sand or wood shavings to flour, or employing small boys to hide under the counter and steal bits of dough brought in by customers for baking.

◀ Bakers' boys used a trap door that opened under the counter to steal bits of dough brought in by customers.

Butchers and blood

Butchers often slaughtered animals behind the shop then just threw the guts and blood out into the street or sometimes into a river. Laws prevented butchers trading by candlelight, as some were guilty of selling rotten meat.

TRUE OR FALSE?
Some stalls ran home deliveries for takeaway foods.

▲ Medieval butchers often threw animal remains out into the street, attracting stray dogs, rats and other pests.

Hunting and hawks

In the Middle Ages, people loved hunting and killing animals for food and sport. Hunters used bows and arrows, crossbows, spears and swords, and chased their prey with the help of horses, dogs and hawks. Dogs were used for hunting larger beasts like boars and deer.

▶ Some women enjoyed hunting too. They used clubs to kill small prey like squirrels.

Terrible traps

Nets and sticky **birdlime** were used to trap birds. Hawks and falcons were often taken from their nests for training. The baby birds had their eyes sewn up so they would not be scared or distracted during training.

▲ Hunters brushed birdlime onto the branches of trees so the birds' feet would stick to it.

The hunter trained them with meat or **lures** then live prey, often birds like herons that had had their legs broken to make the kill easier.

Heads and tails

Medieval recipe books include dishes like baked hedgehog and squirrel, stuffed porpoise stomach, and beavers' tails. For banquets, roast meats such as boar's head and birds, sometimes stuffed one inside another or dressed in their feathers, were popular. They included roast swans, peacocks and bustards (large birds which became extinct because of hunting), as well as smaller birds like gulls, starlings and blackbirds.

▲ King Richard II of England sometimes gave feasts for up to 10,000 guests. At one, cooks prepared 140 hogs, 14 oxen, 12 calves, 12 boars and 3 tonnes of venison.

Castles and Catapults

FACT Many great stone castles were built in the Middle Ages. They were fortified with a castle **keep**, high walls and **ramparts** and often surrounded by a mound or moat to keep out invaders.

▼ Mangonels and trebuchets were giant catapults made with twisted animal guts that fired huge rocks at castle walls. Some were so large they needed twenty men and a team of oxen to move them.

Gruesome truth

Medieval castles were the scene of bloody battles between rival armies raised by kings or nobles.

Cross bows and chain mail

Knights fought with crossbows, longbows, maces, axes and daggers. Maces were long poles with a spiked ball on the end that could be swung around, causing terrible injuries. Ballistas were huge cross bows that could fire rocks or arrows. Longbows fired arrows that could pierce chain mail, and bring a horse down from 180 metres away. Daggers were used for hand to hand fighting. When a man was down, they could be used to kill him by stabbing through the eye slits in his helmet.

▼ To scale the castle walls, attackers used huge ladders or siege towers mounted on wheels. Wet animal skins were used to protect the men from rocks, arrows and boiling oil thrown from the castle ramparts.

WHAT IS IT?

Sheriffs and Stocks

FACT In the Middle Ages, Lords of the Manor had the power to judge and punish small crimes. More serious crimes were punished by shire reeves in shire courts, or by royal judges who travelled the country to hear cases in county courts.

Gruesome truth

Judges could order harsh punishments including cutting off body parts, hanging, beheading or death by burning. For the most serious crimes like **treason**, prisoners could be hanged, drawn and quartered, which meant they were hanged, then their bodies were taken down and the guts pulled out before they were cut into four quarters!

▼ The word 'sheriff' comes from the shire reeves who acted as judges in the Middle Ages.

Gory gibbets

The punishments for theft included having an ear or hand cut off. Violent crimes like murder were punished by death in front of a jeering crowd in a public place. Most towns had **gibbets** where criminals were left hanging until their bodies rotted away, as a warning to others.

◄ People caught poaching animals in royal parks could have their ears cut off as punishment.

Stocks and stools

For smaller crimes, market places had wooden **stocks** or **pillories**, which held criminals prisoner while crowds threw rotten eggs, tomatoes, mud and even dead rats at them. Cheating bakers, nagging women or children who stole apples were punished by putting them on a **ducking stool**, which plunged them into a cold river or pond.

TRUE OR FALSE?
Under Medieval law, animals could be put on trial and punished for crimes just like people.

▶ Prisoners could be forced to stand for three days in the pillory.

Terrible Tortures

FACT In the Middle Ages, torture was sometimes used to get information or confessions, to punish and to take revenge. People could be tortured for being a witch, for **adultery** or murder, and for crimes of **heresy** against the Catholic faith or church.

Gruesome truth

Victims were sometimes tortured for days until they died a slow, agonising death. Some were imprisoned and tortured in underground dungeons and torture chambers. Others were tortured in a public place so spectators could watch their agony.

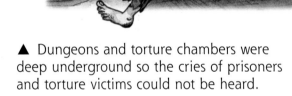

▲ Dungeons and torture chambers were deep underground so the cries of prisoners and torture victims could not be heard.

▼ A prisoner could be tortured in the stocks by having his feet tickled.

Tortures and tickles

Terrifying torture devices included the head crusher, the knee splitter and the foot screw. People could be tortured by being burned, boiled in oil or water, or even tickled! Some were impaled, which meant a sharp pole went right through their body. Others were sawn in half slowly as they hung upside down.

◀ Hanging cages were metal body cages. Prisoners were left to die in them or their dead bodies were hung outside town halls, law courts or palaces as a warning to others.

WHAT IS IT?

▼ Dead bodies left out on a wheel attracted scavenger birds.

The wheel

Some victims were tied to a wheel, which was slowly turned while the torturer broke their bones with a hammer. The wheel was sometimes raised on a pole or platform and they were left to die with birds and animals feeding on their flesh.

Deadly Diseases

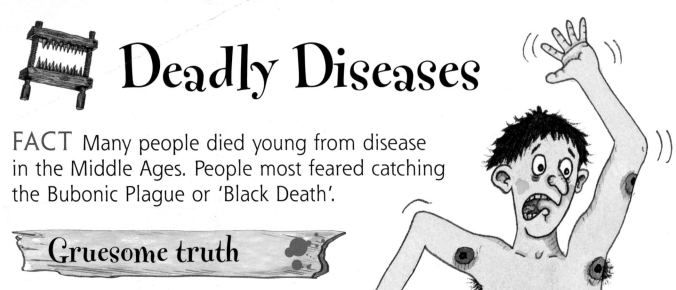

FACT Many people died young from disease in the Middle Ages. People most feared catching the Bubonic Plague or 'Black Death'.

Gruesome truth

The Plague killed one in three people across Europe in the late 1340s. So many died, bodies piled up around mass graves or lay rotting in houses.

▲ The Black Death or Bubonic Plague was named after the black boils or buboes it caused.

▼ So many people died that the bodies had to be buried in mass graves called Plague Pits.

Fleas and fire
The Plague was spread by fleas carried by rats. People caught it from flea bites. The disease caused black boils to swell and fill with pus on the armpits and **groin** and victims vomited and coughed up blood. They could be dead within three days.

Another disease, St. Anthony's Fire, made people go mad, vomit and get terrible burning pains and blood poisoning, which made their toes and fingers, or even their hands and feet, drop off.

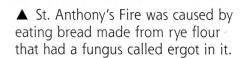

▲ St. Anthony's Fire was caused by eating bread made from rye flour that had a fungus called ergot in it.

Illness and itches

Dirty water made **typhoid** common. Peasants could suffer **scurvy** from a lack of vitamin C in their diets and the rough woollen clothes they wore could cause rashes and skin problems.

▲ In Medieval times, people used water from rivers or streams but often it carried dangerous germs.

TRUE OR FALSE?
People mostly drank ale rather than water in the Middle Ages.

Curious Cures

FACT In the Middle Ages, doctors, **apothecaries** and surgeons treated illness and diseases. Apothecaries made up drugs and herbal remedies and surgeons performed operations including amputations and bone setting, using **anaesthetics** made from plants.

Gruesome truth

Doctors used spells and charms as well as potions made with animal blood, fat and dung. Surgeons used poisons like hemlock and deadly nightshade as anaesthetics and poor hygiene meant that many patients died from infections or blood poisoning.

▼ For toothache, doctors advised wearing a magpie's beak around the neck.

▲ For skin diseases, the patient was told to wear the skin of a wolf, so that the disease would feed on that rather than the patient's skin.

▶ One remedy for gout was a paste of goat's droppings mixed with honey and the herb rosemary.

Blood and prayers

Bloodletting was popular, as bad blood was believed to cause disease. People went to the barber's shop where the barber-surgeon bled them by cutting into a vein. Some barbers kept a bowl of fresh blood in the window.

▼ Barbers worked as surgeons and dentists as well as cutting hair. The red on a barber's pole stood for blood!

WHAT IS IT?

Many ordinary people could not afford to pay a doctor or barber-surgeon. They believed illness was a punishment from God for sins, so they relied on prayer or going on a **pilgrimage** to cure them. Some (called Flagellants) believed the only way to pay for their sins and be cured was to whip themselves until they bled!

27

Prayers and Pardons

FACT The Catholic Church and religion played an important part in people's lives in Europe in the Middle Ages. People prayed in church every week and sometimes went on long pilgrimages to visit shrines and holy places.

Gruesome truth

Many ordinary people lived in fear of hell and the devil. The church taught that sinners who did not show regret and change their bad ways would go to hell. But rich people could pay monks to pray for them, and it was sometimes possible to buy a 'pardon' for sins from the church!

▼ Most people in the Middle Ages could not read or write, but wall paintings and stained glass in churches showed them scary pictures of souls being tortured in hell.

▲ Some fraudsters even robbed graves for human bones that they could pass off as saints' relics.

Grisly relics

Churches and monasteries attracted **pilgrims** by displaying the relics of saints. Relics included everything from a saint's bones and blood to bits of brain, nail clippings, hands and hair. Relics were also traded for money and people often carried them around with them in special bags or pouches. They believed that touching a relic could bring blessings and protection, and even cure them from illness.

Mystery plays

Stories from the Bible were performed as Mystery plays in the streets of towns and cities. The plays carried Christian morals and messages, but they could often contain gory scenes like murders and beheadings.

▼ In a play about a beheading, the actors used a dummy and a bag of animal's blood to make it look real!

Hoods and Heretics

In Medieval Europe, the Catholic Church set up a court called the **Inquisition** to seek out and punish people for the sin of **heresy**. People accused of being heretics by the Inquisition could be arrested, put on trial, tortured and even killed.

▼ Victims of the Inquisition could be chained or walled up and tortured to make them confess to their sins.

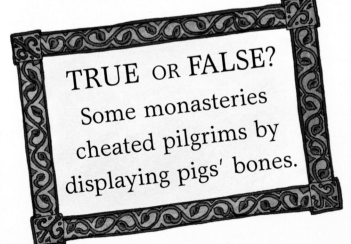

TRUE OR FALSE?
Some monasteries cheated pilgrims by displaying pigs' bones.

Glossary

adultery	being unfaithful or cheating on a married partner
ammonia	chemical solution used for cleaning
anaesthetics	substances that cause temporary unconsciousness
apothecaries	people who prepared remedies and medicines
apprenticed	made a trainee to a trade or craft
birdlime	sticky substance made from plant berries used to catch birds
cesspit	pit for sewage
Cuttlefish	a marine animal from the same family as octopuses.
ducking stool	a stool or chair on a frame that could be worked like a seesaw
feudal	a social system in which a lord has land and power over people in return for protecting them
gibbets	frames for hanging people by their neck from a rope
groin	part of the lower body above the thighs
harrows	farming tools that have teeth or spikes to break up ploughed earth
heresy	the sin of rejecting a religious faith
illuminated manuscript	a manuscript that has words and pictures decorated with gold leaf
Inquisition, the	a legal body that looked into accusations and put people on trial
keep	the innermost and strongest part of a castle
lures	feathered decoys that are swung on a long rope to attract a bird of prey
moat	a wide trench filled with water
pilgrimage	a journey made for a religious purpose
pilgrims	people who go on a pilgrimage
pillories	wooden frames with holes for the head and hands used for criminals
quick lime	chemical compound of calcium
ramparts	mounds of earth with stone or earth defences on top
scurvy	a disease caused by lack of vitamin C
scythes	farming tools with long blades for cutting grain by hand

soul	the spiritual part of a person
stocks	a wooden frame with holes for the hands and feet used for criminals
treason	the crime of plotting against a king, queen or ruler
typhoid	a disease caused by germs carried in water

 # Further Information

Books

The Horrible, Miserable Middle Ages by Kathy Allen, Fact Finders 2011

The Measly Middle Ages by Terry Deary, Scholastic 2007

Weapons of the Middle Ages by Mat Doeden, Blazers 2008

Websites

http://www.historyonthenet.com/Medieval_Life/manor.htm
http://medievaleurope.mrdonn.org/
http://historyforkids.org/learn/medieval/

Places to visit

Warwick Castle
The London Dungeon
The Tower of London

 # Author Note

I have always been fascinated by the Middle Ages. People's lives then were so short and hard yet they produced soaring cathedrals and beautiful works of art. The period that gave us wonderful poetry and the first printed books was also a time of grisly goings-on, from terrible torture devices and horrendous hygiene to deadly weapons and diseases.

Jillian Powell

Index

Answers

Page 7 What is it? A watering pot. These pots were used to sprinkle loose straw with water to keep dust and bugs at bay.

Page 9 What is it? A chamber pot for men to wee into.

Page 11 What is it? A flail. It was used for knocking grain from the stalks for harvest.

Page 13 True or False? False. But they were washed in it! People believed that washing a baby in dirty dishwater would give them strength.

Page 15 True or False? True. Food was delivered in baskets or on barrows.

Page 19 What is it? A leather sword frog, or holder for a sword.

Page 21 True or False? True. An animal could be tried for injuring or killing a person.

Page 23 What is it? A knee splitter: this horrible torture device crushed the victim's knee.

Page 25 True or False? True. It was considered safer to drink than water.

Page 27 What is it? A barber's pole and dish used for blood letting. The patient squeezed the pole to open veins in the arms and the blood dripped down into the dish.

Page 29 True or False? True. Fake relics were also traded for money.